AWFUL DAD JOKES

ANDRE FRANCIS

ANDRE FRANCIS

ISBN: 978-0-473-56733-0 (Paperback)
ISBN: 978-0-473-56734-7 (Hardcover)
ISBN: 978-0-473-56735-4 (Kindle)
ISBN: 978-0-473-56736-1 (PDF)

TABLE OF CONTENTS

TOTALLY AWFUL DAD JOKES 1

Introduction 9

Instructions 10

Dad Jokes 10

Conclusion 97

ANDRE FRANCIS

TOTALLY AWFUL DAD JOKES

© COPYRIGHT 2021 KONNECTD KIDS
ALL RIGHTS RESERVED.

The content contained within this book may not be reproduced, duplicated or transmitted without direct written permission from the author or the publisher.

Under no circumstances will any blame or legal responsibility be held against the publisher, or author, for any damages, reparation, or monetary loss due to the information contained within this book. Either directly or indirectly.

Legal Notice:

This book is copyright protected. This book is only for personal use. You cannot amend, distribute, sell, use, quote or paraphrase any part, or the content within this book, without the consent of the author or publisher.

Disclaimer Notice:

Please note the information contained within this document is for educational and entertainment purposes only. All effort has been executed to present accurate, up to date, and reliable, complete information. No warranties of any kind are declared or implied. Readers acknowledge that the author is not engaging in the rendering of legal, financial, medical or professional advice. The content within this book has been derived from various sources. Please consult a licensed professional before attempting any techniques outlined in this book.

By reading this document, the reader agrees that under no circumstances is the author responsible for any losses, direct or indirect, which are incurred as a result of the use of the information contained within this document, including, but not limited to, — errors, omissions, or inaccuracies.

ANDRE FRANCIS

KONNECTD KIDS
Supply Mechanix LLC
30 N Gould St STE R
Sheridan, Wyoming, 82801
United States of America

www.konnectdkids.com
www.konnectdsupply.com
beawesome@konnectdkids.com
Facebook.com/konnectdkids
Instagram.com/konnectdkids

Illustrations: Marco Angelo Aspera
Edited by Andy Sowden

SPECIAL BONUS!

Get **FREE** Books!

Konnectd Kids creates Joke Books, Colouring Books, Activity books and many more. Hundreds of others are already enjoying insider access to current and future books, 100% free!

If you want insider access all you have to do is **scan the code below or put the link into your web browser** to claim your offer and join the Konnectd Kids Tribe!

https://tinyurl.com/y5rqbqjm

ANDRE FRANCIS

Introduction

The Dad joke is like a universal language that is understood the world over. It doesn't matter which country you come from, every kid has had the experience of growing up with their Dad, Grandad or Uncle telling a Dad Joke, or an attempt at one.

This passing down of Dad jokes from one generation to the next either verbally or in written form is a time honored tradition. Some of these jokes are hilarious, but most of the time they are TOTALLY AWFUL!

I recall as a kid my Dad handing out his puns and one liners, and me groaning loudly at how bad they were. Every now and then there would be one that was simply brilliant, but most of the time, they were totally awful.

My brother and I got to a stage where we would rate the joke, pun or one-liner from one to ten. These jokes from my own Dad has helped inspire this book.

We hope you enjoy this book and use it wisely as the power of Dad jokes is now in your hands.

Instructions

How you want to use this book of Dad Jokes is up to you. You can read them to your family or take turns reading them out.

Why not turn it into a game! A good laugh is best shared, so one suggestion is that you can take turns with different players asking the questions and other family members giving their best shot at answering them.

Whatever way you decide to use these jokes the most important thing is to have a fun no matter how groan worthy the Dad jokes may be.

Enjoy, and have fun.

Did you hear about the bacon cheeseburger who couldn't stop telling jokes?

It was on a roll.

I lost my mood ring...

I can't work out how to feel about it!

My brother drove his new car into a tree...

He found out how his Mercedes bends!

Some animals at the Zoo escaped from the Aquatic Department...

It was Otter chaos!

Long fairy tales...
They tend to drag...on!

What's the difference between a hippo and a Zippo?
A hippo is really heavy, and a Zippo is a little lighter.

Why did the coroner go to the hairdresser?
He heard someone dyed there

TOTALLY AWFUL DAD JOKES

My friend is obsessed with bird watching at night...

He's an owlcoholic!

What did the Prison Librarian think of his job?

It had its pros and 'cons'.

Why did the invisible man turn down the job offer?

He couldn't see himself doing it.

Why don't ants get ill?

It's because they have antibodies.

What is the difference between an alligator and a crocodile?

One will see you later, and the other will see you in a while.

How did the farmer find his wife?

He a-tractor.

What do you call a cow who is good at math?

A Cow-culator.

I am terrified of elevators...

I am going to be taking steps to avoid them!

TOTALLY AWFUL DAD JOKES

What do you call an elephant that no one wants?

An irrelephant.

I had a job predicting lightning storms...

I went on strike!

Whoever invented "Knock-knock" jokes...

should get a no-bell prize!

Why do Chickens not like the Internet?

They prefer book, book, books.

Why did the Dad sell the vacuum cleaner?
Because it was just gathering dust.

Why did the blind man fall into the well?
Because he couldn't see that well.

Who do you call when you break your toe?
A Toe Truck

What do you call a famous dad?
POP star.

TOTALLY AWFUL DAD JOKES

How many tickles does it take to make an octopus laugh?

10 tickles.

What did one Cowboy dad say to the other Cowboy dad?

Live by the pun, die by the Pun.

Did you hear about the greedy clock?

It went back four seconds.

What do you call an ant that has been shunned by his community?

A socially dissed ant.

I'm not going vegetarian...
It'd be a missed steak!

Two cannibals are eating a clown, One says to the other...
"Does this taste funny to you?"

Why do bees have sticky hair?
Because they use Honeycombs.

Did you hear about the guy who invented Lifesavers?
They say he made a mint!

What do you do if you kids want a space themed birthday party?
You plan-et.

Why does a milking stool only have 4 legs?
Because the cow has the udder one.

I fired my electrician...
His work was shocking!

What's brown and sounds like a bell?
Dung!

I was sitting in traffic the other day...

Probably why I got run over!

Why do trees seem suspicious on sunny days?

They just seem a little shady!

A pair of jump leads walk into a pub. The barman tells them...

"I'll serve you, but don't go starting anything."

How many storm troopers does it take to change a lightbulb?

None. Because they are all on the dark side.

Why does Peter Pan always fly?

Because he neverlands!

Why do melons have weddings?

Because they cantaloupe!

I accidentally handed my wife the superglue instead of her lipstick...

She still isn't talking to me!

What do you call a donkey with only three legs?

A wonkey!

I went to the corner shop today...

Bought four corners!

They say that Money can't buy you happiness?

Well, check this out, I bought myself a Happy Meal!

TOTALLY AWFUL DAD JOKES

I wouldn't buy anything with Velcro...
It's a total rip-off!

Would a cardboard belt be...
a waist of paper?

My boss told me to have a good day...
So, I went home!

What do you get from a pampered cow?
Spoiled milk.

How do make a music star out of a chicken?

By making a chicken wrap.

What is so special about a shovel?

It was a ground-breaking invention.

How much does it cost Santa to park his sleigh?

Nothing, it's on the house.

Why can't bikes stand up on their own?

Because they are two tyred.

What do seals do when they are feeling sick?

They Sea Kelp.

Why can't dogs drive cars?

Because they can't move it out of Bark.

Why did the wedding cake need a tissue?

Because it was in tiers.

What do scientists freshen their breath with?

With experi-mints!

What was Beethoven's favourite fruit?

The ba-na-na-n

What did the mother broom say to the baby broom?

It was time to go to sweep.

How does the moon cut its hair?

Eclipse it.

TOTALLY AWFUL DAD JOKES

What rock group has four men that don't sing?
Mount Rushmore.

What time did the man go to the dentist?
Tooth hurt-y.

My Gardener did a terrible job and I wanted my money back...
He said I should speak to the 'branch' manager!

Without geometry....
Life is pointless

A computer once beat me at chess...
But it was no match for me at kickboxing!

I quit my job today as a sign writer...
I could see the writing on the wall!

I just quit my job at Starbucks because day after day...
It was the same old grind!

My co-worker told a terrible granny smith joke...
It was appalling!

TOTALLY AWFUL DAD JOKES

A burger walks into a bar...

The bartender says, "sorry sir we don't serve food here".

Why did the coffee file a police report?

It got mugged.

Why was the cookie very sad?
It was feeling crumby.

What's the difference between a badly dressed man on a tricycle and a well-dressed man on a bicycle?
Attire.

How much does a hipster weigh?
An Instagram.

What kind of a car does an egg drive?
A Yolkswagen.

Dad, can you put the Cat out?
I didn't know it was on fire.

Did you hear about the kidnapping at Pre-School?
It's fine, he woke up.

Why did the green lettuce blush?
It saw the salad dressing.

What day do you watch the Thor movies?
Thors'day.

What is brown and sticky?
A stick.

What time is it?
I don't know. It keeps changing.

Don't you just hate it when people answer their own questions?
I do.

TOTALLY AWFUL DAD JOKES

What did the vegetarian priest say to the crowd?

Lettuce pray!

What are you doing if you arrange squirrels by height?

You are critter-sizing.

What do you call someone who sees an Apple store get robbed?

An iWitness.

Have you heard about the Italian chef who died?

He pasta away.

People say I am stubborn...

But I never believe them!

What do you call a fly without wings?

A walk.

What did the policeman say to his belly button?

You're under a vest!

I saw an ad for burial plots, and thought to myself...

This is the last thing I need!

In the Queens Gambit TV Show you see chess players in a hotel reception going on about how good they are...

They were chess-nuts boasting in an open foyer!

Why do you never hear a psychiatrist go to the toilet?

Because the 'P' is silent.

What is so good about the earth rotating?

It makes my day!

What did the fish say when he hit the wall?

Dam.

Why is it so hard to work out what species birds are?

Because they are always in da-skies.

If at first you don't succeed...

Skydiving is not for you!

How many contractors does it take to change a lightbulb?

Ohhhhhhh, hard to say, looks like a big job, when we get the light bulb out, could be all sorts of problems.

Do you know the story about the chicken that crossed the Mexican border?

Me neither, I couldn't follow it.

What does a house wear?

A dress.

As a lumberjack I know I have chopped down 3,123 trees. How you ask?

Every time I chop one down, I keep a log.

TOTALLY AWFUL DAD JOKES

What do you call someone who steps on a cornflake?
Cereal killer.

What do you call a Mexican whose vehicle has been stolen?
Carlos.

How do you make a handkerchief dance?
You put a little boogie in it.

"What did Mississippi let Delaware?"
"I don't know, but Alaska!

Why do bees hum?
Because they don't know the words.

What's the best smelling insect?
A deodar-ant.

How do you help a crocodile if it gets injured?
Give it Gatorade.

Did you hear about the guy who stole calendars?
He got 12 months.

TOTALLY AWFUL DAD JOKES

**I was wondering
"Why does a frisbee appear larger
the closer it gets?"**
And then it hit me!

**What do you call the
graveyard in town?**
The dead centre of town.

**I can't stop stealing.
Sometimes when it gets really bad...**
I take something for it!

**What is the cutest creature
in the sea?**
A cuddlefish.

What birds do you find in Portugal?
Portugeese.

Why didn't the two roosters cross the road?
They were two chicken.

A cartoonist has been found dead...
The details are sketchy!

What does a vegetarian zombie eat?
GRA-A-A-A-A-I-I-I-I-N-N-N-S-S

How can you spot a dogwood tree?
By its Bark!

What did the mathematician say to the person who created the zero?
Thanks for nothing.

What did the picture say to the wall?
First they frame me than they hang me.

What happens when you make too many right hand turns in life?
You'll get dizzy.

What type of bagel can fly?
A plane bagel.

Why do some couples go to the gym?
Because some relationships don't work out.

TOTALLY AWFUL DAD JOKES

Why is it terrible to work in a shoe recycling shop?
Because it is sole destroying.

Why did the angler dress up in a suit to go fishing?
He was fishing for a compliment.

Dad, did you get a haircut?
No, I got them all cut!

Why don't roofs sing?
They're too pitchy.

Why do scuba divers fall backwards out of the boat?

Because if they fall frontwards...they'd still be in the boat.

What language do dandruff speak?

Hairbrew!

Which Spice Girl can carry the most petrol?

Geri can.

Why did the math book look so sad?

Because of all of its problems!

What did the computer go to the doctor?

Because he had a virus!

Which U.S. state is famous for it's extra-small soft drinks?

Minnesota!

How does a computer learn something?

Bit, by bit, by bit.

Why do doctors hit people knees with their little hammer?

Because they get a kick out of it.

TOTALLY AWFUL DAD JOKES

How does a Penguin make a house for itself?
Igloos it together.

What did the ocean say to the seashore?
Nothing, it gave a big wave!

What happens if you punch a frequency?
It Hertz!

I'd like to give a big shout out to all the sidewalks...
For keeping me off the streets!

I named my horse Mayo...

Mayo neighs!

When does an arborist finish work?

At tree o'clock.

Did you hear about the cannibal who threw a pile of funny bones into a boiling pot?

He made himself a laughingstock.

Which country's capital city has the fastest-growing population?

Ireland. Every day it's Dublin.

TOTALLY AWFUL DAD JOKES

Why did the can crusher quit his job?
Because it was soda pressing!

Which state has the most streets?
Rhode Island.

What do you call cheese that isn't yours?
Nacho cheese.

How do you get a squirrel to like you?
Act like a nut.

Did you hear that McDonalds now have burgers patties made from insects?

They call it a Hoppy Meal.

What do you call an airplane with no wings?

Air Plain.

Did you know diarrhea is hereditary?

It runs in your genes.

Are you ready for the zoom meeting?

Not even remotely.

What's orange and sounds like a Parrot?

A carrot!

How do you light up a football stadium?

With a football match.

Why are spiders so smart?

They can find everything on the web.

I was going to tell a time-traveling joke...

But you guys didn't like it!

What did the left eye say to the right eye?

Between us, something smells.

Did you hear about the explosion at the cheese factory?

There was de brie everywhere!

How do caterpillars swim?

Using the butterfly stroke.

TOTALLY AWFUL DAD JOKES

What do you call a man who can't stand up?

Neil.

What do you call a sink with a dutch shoe in it?

A clogged sink.

What did the fisherman say to the magician?

Pick a cod, any cod.

Why is having a cross eyed teacher an issue?

Because she can't control her pupils.

Which is faster, hot or cold?

Hot, because you can catch a cold.

When I was a kid, my Dad told me I could be anyone I wanted to be...

Turns out, identity theft is a crime!

Why did the baker steal a mixer from work?

It was a whisk he was willing to take.

I left my job as a smartphone reviewer...

I wasn't comparing apples with apples!

What do you call it when a hen looks at a lettuce?

A chicken ceasar salad.

What do you call a Dad joke that no one laughs at?

A Dead joke.

What happens to an illegally parked frog?

It gets Toad.

What's a Dads favourite chair?

A recliner, it's because they go way back.

TOTALLY AWFUL DAD JOKES

Why did the egg have a day off?
because it was Fryday.

Why is Saturday stronger than Wednesday?
Wednesday is a week day.

How do Lawyers say goodbye?
We'll be suing ya!

What do scholars eat when they're hungry?
Academia nuts.

Why did the boy eat his homework?
Because his teacher said it was a piece of cake.

What is a cannibals favourite food?
Raw-men.

What do you call a really fat psychic?
A four chin teller.

Why is making a diamond shaped like a duck a bad idea?
It quacks under pressure.

TOTALLY AWFUL DAD JOKES

Why was the cheese sad?
Because it was Blue!

Why did the pony ask for a glass of water?
Because he was a little horse.

What is a cat's favourite pizza?
Purrrrperoni.

Why was the graveyard overcrowded?
Because people are dying to get there.

ANDRE FRANCIS

Can February March?
No, but April May.

Did you hear about the cafe on the moon?
Great food, no atmosphere.

What do you call a woman who sounds like an ambulance?
Nin

Want to hear my pizza joke?
Never mind, it's too cheesy.

TOTALLY AWFUL DAD JOKES

What do you call an alligator wearing a vest?

An investi-gator.

What do you call someone with no body and no nose?

Nobody knows.

What word can you make shorter by adding two letters?

Short!

What did the scarf say to the hat?

"You hang around here, I'll go on ahead".

Why are skeletons so calm?

Because nothing gets under their skin!

After dinner, I was asked if I could clear the table...

I needed a run up, but I made it!

I just finished making my first bookcase...

I'm very proud of my shelf!

What do you call pie?

Yummy.

TOTALLY AWFUL DAD JOKES

What are a bee's favourite neckless made from?

Bee-ds.

Hey is your refrigerator running?

You better go catch it.

I quit my job as an upholsterer...

It wouldn't cover the bills...

Elvis Presley couldn't write a song after experiencing an earthquake...

He was all shook up!

What fish can you use to make your car go faster?

A tuna

What did one light bulb say to the other at a party?

"This party's lit".

What did the janitor say when he jumped out of the broom closet?

Supplies!!!!

TOTALLY AWFUL DAD JOKES

What is it, when you have a bear with no teeth?

A Gummy Bear!

What has four wheels and flies?

A: A garbage truck!

Why did the scarecrow win an award?

Because he was outstanding in his field.

I ate a clock today...

It was very time-consuming!

Why don't eggs tell jokes?

They'd crack each other up.

Why did the turkey cross the road TWICE?

To prove he wasn't a chicken.

What do you call a rabbit with fleas?

"bugs" bunny.

Why did the chicken cross the road?

It was bored of just standing there.

What do Santa's elves listen to as they work?

Wrap music!

How many South Americans does it take to change a lightbulb?
A Brazilian.

I quit my job at the swing factory...
All day long, it was backward and forward!

Over Easter the police helicopter was circling our neighbourhood...
They were looking for some bad eggs!

Did you hear about the man who was sacked from the calendar factory?
He took a couple of days off.

TOTALLY AWFUL DAD JOKES

Why do seagulls fly over the ocean?
Because if they flew over the bay we'd call them bagels.

What happened when you go on a tropical food diet?
It makes a mango crazy.

What Happened to the boiling water?
It will be mist.

Why are bananas good at drag racing?
Because they like to peel out of places.

What do you call the boss at Old MacDonald's Farm?

The CIEIO

What would you call Thor if he wrote a novel?

an Au-Thor

Why don't skeletons ever go trick or treating?

Because they have no body to go with.

I hate Russian dolls...

They're so full of themselves!

Did you hear about the circus fire?
It was in tents.

What do you call a man with a seagull on his head?
You call him 'Cliff.'

Why do crabs never give to charity?
Because they're shellfish.

Why didn't the skeleton climb the mountain?
It didn't have the guts!

Why did the whale cross the harbour?

To get to the other tide.

What happens when a drummer comes out of retirement?

There are repercussions.

Have you ever seen me tie my shoelaces with my mind?

I thought knot

What's a foot long and slippery?

A slipper.

TOTALLY AWFUL DAD JOKES

Guess what I saw?
Wood

One of my favorite memories as a kid was when my Dad used to put me inside a tire and roll me down a hill...
They were Goodyears!

I have a Black Hole joke...
But it's kind of dark and goes on forever!

Where do baby cats learn to swim?
The kitty pool.

What did one wall say to the other?

I'll meet you at the corner.

Why did the lollipop store close down?

They lost their licker license.

Why did the elephant stand on the marshmallow?

So he wouldn't fall into the hot chocolate.

How can a leopard change his spots?

By moving.

TOTALLY AWFUL DAD JOKES

I just found out I'm color-blind...
The diagnosis came completely out of the purple!

Did you hear the rumor about butter?
Well, I'm not going to spread it!

Where do you see yourself in 5 years?
In a mirror.

What did the tomato say to the other tomato during a race?
You had better Ketch up.

What did the guy say when he got caught downloading the entire Wikipedia?

I can explain everything.

What is a witches favorite topic?

Spelling!

Why shouldn't you eat Sushi?

It's a little bit fishy

What's an astronaut's favorite part of a computer?

The SPACE bar.

TOTALLY AWFUL DAD JOKES

Why are snakes measured in inches?
Because they don't have any feet.

What did Hannibal Lecter call his imaginary friend?
Stu.

Where did the general keep his armies?
In his Sleevies!

Want to hear a joke about construction?
Nah, I'm still working on it.

What do you call it when you go drifting in a Tesla?

Electric slide.

What did the baby corn say to the mama corn?

Where's POP corn?

Why can't you hear a pterodactyl using the bathroom?

Because the P is silent.

Dogs can't operate MRI machines...

But cats can!

Why can't a nose be 12 inches long?

Because then it would be a foot.

Why do chicken coops have two doors?

Because if they had four doors, they'd be chicken sedans.

What did the sushi say to the bee?
Wasabi!

What's the best way to watch a fly-fishing tournament?
Live stream.

What's the heaviest soup in Asia?
One ton.

Dad "What's the difference between a piano, a tuna, and a pot of glue? Kid "I don't know"?

You can tuna piano, but you can't piano a tun

Kid "What about the glue?

Dad "I knew you would get stuck there"

What's the quickest way to double your money?

Fold it in half.

We are working on a dad joke about hurricanes...

When we are done you'll be blown away!

I think I married a secret agent,

she is always sleeping in... she must be a sleeper agent!

What's Forrest Gump's Facebook password?

1forest1

How do you tell the difference between a bull and a milk cow?

It is either one or the udder.

How do celebrities stay cool?

They have many fans.

TOTALLY AWFUL DAD JOKES

What do you call someone who moves beehives in America?
A US Bee driver.

Son: Dad, how does it feel to have an amazing son?
Dad: I don't know, ask your grandfather!

Did you hear about the electric eel who went to the hospital?
She was discharged.

What do you call a pile of cats?
A meowtain.

Why was the broom late for work?

It overswept!

Why can't a leopard hide?

Because he's always spotted.

TOTALLY AWFUL DAD JOKES

Why can you trust a walrus to keep a secret?

Because his lips are sealed.

I'm so good at sleeping...

I can do it with my eyes closed!

Why should you not do dad jokes about retired people?

None of them work.

Why are elevator jokes so good?

They work on so many levels.

Did you know that Davy Crockett had three ears?

His left ear, his right ear and his wild frontier.

What kind of fish is made of only 2 sodium atoms?

2 Na

My friend says to me, "What rhymes with orange?"

And I told him, "No it doesn't!"

What do you call a cow with a twitch?

Beef jerky.

What is a hairdresser's favourite food?

Barber-que of course.

What did the pirate say on his 80th birthday?

Aye matey!

Did I tell you the time I fell in love during a backflip?

I was heels overhead.

Someone said to me today that they don't understand Cloning...

I told him, that makes 2 of us!

Have you heard about these amazing new property investment opportunities in Egypt?

Don't do it, it's a pyramid scheme.

What do you call an eyeless fish?

Fsh.

Time flies like an arrow...

Fruit flies like a banana!

Have you heard about the chocolate record player?

It sounds pretty sweet.

What do you call a Cowboy Dad?

A Punslinger!

What do you call a super articulate dinosaur?

A Thesaurus.

Why are dogs horrible dancers?
Because they have two left feet!

How was Rome split in two?
With a pair of Caesar's.

What does a baby computer call its father?
Dat

Why are colds bad criminals?
Because they're easy to catch.

TOTALLY AWFUL DAD JOKES

What grades did the pirate get on his report card?
Seven Cs

When is a door not really a door?
When it's really ajar.

Why do vampires seem sick?
They're always coffin.

I was addicted to the hokey pokey...
But thankfully, I turned myself around!

What does a storm cloud wear under his raincoat?

Thunderwear.

What would you get if you'd put a lawyer in a suit?

A lawsuit.

How does a cucumber get into a pickle?

It goes through a jarring experience.

What are two structures that hold water?

Well, Damn...I just can't think of any.

TOTALLY AWFUL DAD JOKES

I just flew in from New York...
And boy are my arms tired!

I told my mom I was going to make a car out of spaghetti...
you should have seen her face when I drove straight pasta!

I made a Dad joke and I am not a Dad...
Does that make me a faux pa?

"Dad, please make me a sandwich."

"Poof! You're a sandwich!"

Conclusion

Our mission at Konnectd Kids is to ensure you and your family have fun and that with the help of our books that you turn these fun experiences into remarkable memories!

Author Andre Francis has worked to create and collate a collection of jokes that we hoped you thoroughly enjoyed. Our *'Totally Awful Dad Jok*es' book was made specifically to share the fun and the humor from great, good, and terribly awful Dad jokes

Thank you for the interest in this book and we invite you to take a look at our Konnectd Kids Publishing catalogue for any other books that may be of interest at www.konnectdkids.com

My final request...

Being a smaller publisher, reviews help us tremendously!

It would mean the world to me if you could leave a review by going to the link below.

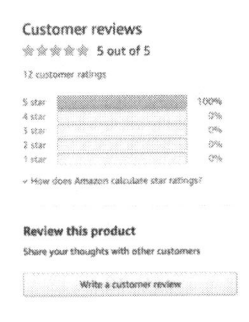

If you or your kids enjoyed this book, then please go to this link that will take you to Amazon to leave a review

www.konnectdkids.com/review

It only takes 30 seconds but means so much to me!

Thank you and I can't wait to see your thoughts.

Visit us at:
www.konnectdkids.com

Our Books and Products:
www.konnectdkids.com/books
www.konnectdsupply.com
www.etsy.com/shop/konnectd
konnectd.redbubble.com

Find us on Instagram
@Konnectdkids

Follow us on Facebook
facebook.com/Konnectdkids

Join our Facebook Group
(Free Books and giveaways)
https://www.facebook.com/groups/konnectdkidsgroup

SPECIAL BONUS!

Get **FREE** Books!

Konnectd Kids creates Joke Books, Colouring Books, Activity books and many more. Hundreds of others are already enjoying insider access to current and future books, 100% free!

If you want insider access all you have to do is **scan the code below or put the link into your web browser** to claim your offer and join the Konnectd Kids Tribe!

https://tinyurl.com/y5rqbqjm

Made in the USA
Coppell, TX
19 November 2023

24481270R00057